A gift for

_____

From

_____

Date

_____

GRACE
FOR THE MOMENT
for Moms

MAX LUCADO

THOMAS NELSON
Since 1798

God thinks you're wonderful!
By the way, Mom,
I think you're wonderful too!

Abba,

You are the Creator of life, and you have gifted me with the precious lives of my children. Please bring light and joy to my world today. The future is filled with the unknown, but help me remember that nothing is unknown to you. When my mind strays to anxious thoughts, light a path for me back to your peace.

Fill my home with your presence, my mind with your wisdom, and my heart with your love. Guide me as I seek to guide my children as they learn to trust in you. Cover them with your hand of protection.

Thank you for hearing my prayers. Thank you for listening as my children pray—those whispered words they say before bed, so often funny and always heartfelt, that make my heart sing. Thank you for putting them in my life.

In Christ's name, amen.

Day 1

God Is Crazy About You

*T*here are many reasons God saved you: to bring glory to himself, to appease his justice, to demonstrate his sovereignty. But one of the sweetest reasons God saved you is because he is fond of you. He likes having you around. He thinks you are the best thing to come down the pike in quite a while.

If God had a refrigerator, your picture would be on it. If he had a wallet, your photo would be in it. He sends you flowers every spring and a sunrise every morning. Whenever you want to talk, he'll listen. He can live anywhere in the universe, and he chose your heart.

Face it, friend. He's crazy about you.

God made galaxies no one has ever seen and dug canyons we have yet to find. And yet he has never taken his eyes off you. Not for a millisecond.

"God even knows how many
hairs are on your head."

MATTHEW 10:30

"God loved the world so much that he gave his
one and only Son so that whoever believes in
him may not be lost, but have eternal life."

JOHN 3:16

Christ's love is greater than anyone can ever know,
but I pray that you will be able to know that love.
Then you can be filled with the fullness of God.

EPHESIANS 3:19

The next time a
sunrise steals your
breath or a meadow
of flowers leaves

you speechless,
remain that way. Say
nothing and listen
as heaven whispers,
"Do you like it? I
did it just for you."

Day 2

Perfected

*W*ith one sacrifice he made perfect forever those who are being made holy" (Hebrews 10:14).

Underline the word *perfect*. Note that the word is not *better*. Not *improving*. Not *on the upswing*. God doesn't improve; he perfects. He doesn't enhance; he completes.

Now, I realize that there's a sense in which we're imperfect. We still err. We still stumble. We still do exactly what we don't want to do. And that part of us is, according to the verse, "being made holy."

Motherhood comes with so many doubts and questionings. But when it comes to our position before God, there is no doubt and no question: you're perfect. When he sees you, he sees one who has been made perfect through the one who is perfect—Jesus Christ.

God does what we cannot do so we can be what
we dare not dream: perfect before God.

"My grace is enough for you. When you are weak, my power is made perfect in you."

2 CORINTHIANS 12:9

With one sacrifice he made perfect forever those who are being made holy.

HEBREWS 10:14

Where God's love is, there is no fear, because God's perfect love drives out fear.

1 JOHN 4:18

God always rejoices when we dare to dream. In fact, he wrote the book on making the impossible possible.

My Prayer

The Beauty Around You

With one decision, history began. Existence became measurable. Out of nothing came light.

Out of light came day.

Then came sky . . . and earth.

And on this earth? A mighty hand went to work.

Canyons were carved. Oceans were dug. Mountains erupted out of flatlands. Stars were flung. A universe sparkled.

Look to the canyons to see the Creator's splendor. Touch the flowers and see his delicacy. Listen to the thunder and hear his power.

Today you will encounter God's creation. When you see the beauty around you, let each detail remind you to lift your head in praise. Express your appreciation for God's creation. Encourage those he has entrusted to you to see the beauty of his creation.

Through his power all things were made—things
in heaven and on earth, things seen and unseen.

COLOSSIANS 1:16

The heavens declare the glory of God, and the
skies announce what his hands have made.

PSALM 19:1

But ask the animals, and they will teach you, or ask
the birds of the air, and they will tell you. Speak to
the earth, and it will teach you, or let the fish of the
sea tell you. Every one of these knows that the hand
of the LORD has done this. The life of every creature
and the breath of all people are in God's hand.

JOB 12:7-10

God will load your world with flowers. He hard delivers a bouquet to your door every day. Open it! Take them!

God Is Listening

*W*hen you wonder if anyone is listening, know this: God is. Your voice matters in heaven. He takes you very seriously. When you enter his presence, he turns to you to hear your voice. No need to fear that you will be ignored. Even if you stammer or stumble, even if what you have to say impresses no one, it impresses God, and he listens. He listens to the painful plea of the elderly in the rest home. He listens to the confession of the prodigal. When the guilty beg for mercy, when the spouse seeks guidance, when the mom steps out of the chaos and into the chapel, God listens.

Intently. Carefully.

God is standing on the front porch of heaven,
expectantly hoping, searching the horizon for a glimpse
of his child. . . . And the name he calls is yours.

Because he turned his ear to me, I
will call on him as long as I live.

PSALM 116:2 NIV

When a believing person prays,
great things happen.

JAMES 5:16

"You will call my name. You will come to me
and pray to me, and I will listen to you. You
will search for me. And when you search for
me with all your heart, you will find me!"

JEREMIAH 29:12–13

Wherever you
want to talk,
God will listen.

Tug-of-War

There is only so much sand in the hourglass. Who gets it?

You know what I'm talking about, don't you?

"The PTA needs a new treasurer. With your background and experience and talent and wisdom and love for kids and degree in accounting, *you* are the perfect one for the job!"

It's tug-of-war, and you are the rope.

"Blessed are the meek," Jesus said. The word *meek* does not mean weak. It means focused. It is a word used to describe a domesticated stallion. Power under control.

Blessed are those who acknowledge that there is only one God and have quit applying for his position. Blessed are those who know what on earth they are on earth to do and set themselves about the business of doing it.

Those who matter most don't want you for what you
can do for them; they want you for who you are.

Each of you has received a gift
to use to serve others.

1 PETER 4:10

"Seek first God's kingdom and what God wants.
Then all your other needs will be met as well."

MATTHEW 6:33

Do you think I am trying to make people accept
me? No, God is the One I am trying to please.
Am I trying to please people? If I still wanted to
please people, I would not be a servant of Christ.

GALATIANS 1:10

A Mother's Care

*I*t all happened in a most remarkable moment . . . a moment like no other.

God became a man. Divinity arrived. Heaven opened itself and placed its most precious one in a human womb.

The omnipotent, in one instant, became flesh and blood. The one who was larger than the universe became a microscopic embryo. And he who sustains the world with a word chose to be dependent upon the nourishment of a young girl.

God had come near—and placed himself in a mother's care.

You play no small part, because there is no small part to be played. God entrusted your part to you alone.

He gave up his place with God and
made himself nothing. He was born
as a man and became like a servant.

PHILIPPIANS 2:7

She will give birth to a son, and you
will name him Jesus, because he will
save his people from their sins.

MATTHEW 1:21

You know the grace of our Lord Jesus
Christ. You know that Christ was rich,
but for you he became poor so that by his
becoming poor you might become rich.

2 CORINTHIANS 8:9

How wide is God's love?
Wide enough for the
whole world. Are you
included in the world?
Then you are
included in
God's love.

My Prayer

_____

_____

_____

_____

_____

_____

_____

_____

_____

_____

Day 7

Chosen

*D*o you ever feel unnoticed? New clothes and styles may help for a while. But if you want permanent change, learn to see yourself as God sees you: "He has covered me with clothes of salvation and wrapped me with a coat of goodness, like a bridegroom dressed for his wedding, like a bride dressed in jewels" (Isaiah 61:10).

Does your self-esteem ever sag? When it does, remember what you are worth. "You were bought, not with something that ruins like gold or silver, but with the precious blood of Christ, who was like a pure and perfect lamb" (1 Peter 1:18–19).

You are chosen.

The challenge is to remember that. To meditate on it. To focus on it. To allow God's love to change the way you look at you.

Since you are God's idea, you are a good idea.

You are a chosen people, royal priests, a holy nation, a people for God's own possession.

1 PETER 2:9

She gave this name to the LORD who spoke to her: "You are the God who sees me," for she said, "I have now seen the One who sees me."

GENESIS 16:13 NIV

You saw my body as it was formed. All the days planned for me were written in your book before I was one day old.

PSALM 139:16

God loves
you simply
because he
has chosen to do
so. He loves
you. Personally.
Powerfully.
Passionately.

Don't Worry

We worry. We worry about the IRS and the SAT and the PTA. We worry that we won't have enough money. And when we have money, we worry that we won't manage it well. We worry that the world will end before the parking meter expires. We worry what the dog thinks if he sees us step out of the shower. We worry that someday we'll learn that fat-free yogurt was fattening.

Honestly, now. Did God save you so you would fret? Would he teach you to walk just to watch you fall? Would he be nailed to the cross for your sins and then disregard your prayers? Come on. Is Scripture teasing us when it says, "He has put his angels in charge of you to watch over you wherever you go" (Psalm 91:11)?

No, I don't think so either.

Though mind-numbingly mighty, he comes in the soft of night and touches us with the tenderness of an April snow. He is the shepherd who loves you.

Don't worry about anything; instead,
pray about everything.

PHILIPPIANS 4:6 NLT

Give your worries to the LORD, and
he will take care of you.

PSALM 55:22

"I leave you peace; my peace I give you. I do
not give it to you as the world does. So don't
let your hearts be troubled or afraid."

JOHN 14:27

With God's power working in us, God can do much,
much more than anything we can ask or imagine.

EPHESIANS 3:20

Day 9

Love Is All You'll Find

*W*ater must be wet. A fire must be hot. You can't take the wet out of water and still have water. You can't take the heat out of fire and still have fire.

In the same way, you can't take the love out of God and still have him exist. For he was . . . and is . . . love.

Probe deep within him. Explore every corner. Search every angle. Love is all you find. Go to the beginning of every decision he has made, and you'll find it. Go to the end of every story he has told, and you'll see it.

Love.

No bitterness. No evil. No cruelty. Just love. Flawless love. Passionate love. Vast and pure love. He is love.

God will love you. Always. No matter what.

We know the love that God has for
us, and we trust that love.

1 JOHN 4:16

"I loved you as the Father loved me.
Now remain in my love."

JOHN 15:9

We love because God first loved us.

1 JOHN 4:19

The Master Decorator

*G*od loves to decorate. God *has* to decorate. Let him live long enough in a heart, and that heart will begin to change. Portraits of hurt will be replaced by landscapes of grace. Walls of anger will be demolished and shaky foundations restored. God can no more leave a life unchanged than a mother can leave her child's tear untouched.

This might explain some of the discomfort in your life. Remodeling of the heart is not always pleasant. We don't object when the Carpenter adds a few shelves, but he's been known to gut the entire west wing. He has such high aspirations for you. God envisions a complete restoration. He won't stop until he is finished. He wants you to be the best you. He wants you to be just like Jesus.

**When will God stop working on you?
When he sees his reflection in you.**

You will know that God's power is
very great for us who believe.

EPHESIANS 1:19

Create in me a pure heart, O God, and
renew a steadfast spirit within me.

PSALM 51:10 NIV

God is working in you to help you want to
do and be able to do what pleases him.

PHILIPPIANS 2:13

Never miss
a chance to read
a child a story.

My Prayer

Day 11

Don't Miss God's Answer

The God of surprises strikes again. God does that for the faithful. Just when the womb gets too old for babies, Sarai gets pregnant. Just when the failure is too great for grace, David is pardoned.

The lesson? Three words. Don't give up.

Is the road long? Don't stop.

Is the night black? Don't quit.

God is watching. For all you know, right at this moment, the check may be in the mail.

The apology may be in the making.

The wandering child may be taking that first step back toward home.

Don't quit. For if you do, you may miss the answer to your prayers.

You have captured the heart of God.
He cannot bear to live without you.

"Is anything too hard for the Lord? No!"

GENESIS 18:14

I know that you can do all things; no
purpose of yours can be thwarted.

JOB 42:2 NIV

Let us hold firmly to the hope that we
have confessed, because we can trust
God to do what he promised.

HEBREWS 10:23

If something is
important to you,
it's important
to God.

God's Child

*L*et me tell you who you are. In fact, let me proclaim who you are.

You are an heir of God and a coheir with Christ
   (Romans 8:17 NIV).
You are eternal, like an angel (Luke 20:36).
You have a crown that will last forever (1 Corinthians 9:25).
You are a holy priest (1 Peter 2:5), a treasured possession
   (Exodus 19:5 NIV).

But more than any of the above—more significant than any title or position—is the simple fact that you are God's child.

You can be everything God wants you to be.

The Father has loved us so much
that we are called children of God.
And we really are his children.

1 JOHN 3:1

For we are God's handiwork, created in
Christ Jesus to do good works, which God
prepared in advance for us to do.

EPHESIANS 2:10 NIV

To all who did accept him and believe in him
he gave the right to become children of God.

JOHN 1:12

Wondering

*T*he white space between Bible verses is fertile soil for questions. One can hardly read Scripture without whispering, "I wonder..."

"I wonder if Eve ever ate any more fruit."

"I wonder if Noah slept well during storms."

But in our wonderings, there are questions we never need to ask: Does God care? Do we matter to God? Does he still love his children?

Through the small face of the stable-born baby, he says yes.

Yes, your sins are forgiven.

Yes, your name is written in heaven.

And yes, God has entered your world. Immanuel. God is with you—and he cares.

It may be difficult for you to believe that God knows your name . . . but he does. Written on his hand. Spoken by his mouth. Whispered by his lips. Your name.

She will have a son, and they will name him
Immanuel, which means "God is with us."

MATTHEW 1:23

"See, I have written your name on my hand."

ISAIAH 49:16

The LORD himself will go before you. He will be
with you; he will not leave you or forget you.

DEUTERONOMY 31:8

Precious Prayers

*Y*ou and I live in a loud world. To get someone's attention is no easy task. They must be willing to set everything aside to listen: turn down the radio, turn away from the monitor, turn the corner of the page and set down the book. When someone is willing to silence everything else so they can hear us clearly, it is a privilege. A rare privilege, indeed.

Your prayers are honored in heaven as precious jewels. Purified and empowered, the words rise in a delightful fragrance to our Lord. Your words do not stop until they reach the very throne of God.

Your prayer on earth activates God's power in heaven, and God's will is done "on earth as it is in heaven" (Matthew 6:10 NIV).

Your prayers move God to change the world. You may not understand the mystery of prayer. You don't need to. But this much is clear: many actions in heaven begin with precious prayers on earth.

The Lord sees the good people
and listens to their prayers.

1 PETER 3:12

In my trouble I called to the Lord. I cried out
to my God for help. From his temple he heard
my voice; my call for help reached his ears.

PSALM 18:6

"I will provide for their needs before they ask, and I
will help them while they are still asking for help."

ISAIAH 65:24

The power of prayer is in the One who hears it and not in the one who says it. Your prayers do make a difference.

A Work in Progress

*G*od is not finished with you yet. Oh, you may think he is. You may think you've peaked. You may think he has someone else to do the job.

If so, think again.

"God began doing a good work in you, and I am sure he will continue it until it is finished when Jesus Christ comes again" (Philippians 1:6).

Did you see what God is doing? *A good work in you.*

Did you see when he will be finished? *When Jesus comes again.*

May I spell out the message? *God ain't finished with you yet.*

God is often more patient with us
than we are with ourselves.

Jesus will keep you strong until the end so
that there will be no wrong in you on the
day our Lord Jesus Christ comes again.

1 CORINTHIANS 1:8

The LORD will fulfill his purpose for me; your
steadfast love, O LORD, endures forever.

PSALM 138:8 ESV

Let us look only to Jesus, the One who began
our faith and who makes it perfect.

HEBREWS 12:2

Thinking of You

*H*eaven knows no difference between Sunday morning and Wednesday afternoon. God longs to speak as clearly in the workplace as he does in the sanctuary. He longs to be worshiped when we sit at the dinner table and not just when we come to his Communion table. You may go days without thinking of him, but there's never a moment when he's not thinking of you.

Knowing this, we can fathom why Paul urged us to "pray without ceasing" (1 Thessalonians 5:17 ESV), "be constant in prayer" (Romans 12:12 ESV), and "let heaven fill your thoughts" (Colossians 3:2 TLB).

Because heaven is thinking of you.

God's thoughts of you outnumber the grains
of sand on the shore. You never leave his mind,
escape his sight, flee his thoughts.

God, your thoughts are precious to me. They
are so many! If I could count them, they
would be more than all the grains of sand.

PSALM 139:17–18

"I know what I am planning for you," says the
LORD. "I have good plans for you, not plans to hurt
you. I will give you hope and a good future."

JEREMIAH 29:11

The LORD directs the steps of the godly. He delights in
every detail of their lives. Though they stumble, they
will never fall, for the LORD holds them by the hand.

PSALM 37:23–24 NLT

God does more than forgive our mistakes: he removes them! We simply have to take them to him.

My Prayer

Day 17

"Come!"

God is an inviting God. He invited Mary to birth his Son, the disciples to fish for men, the adulterous woman to start over, and Thomas to touch his wounds. God is the King who prepares the palace, sets the table, and invites his subjects to come in.

In fact, it seems his favorite word is *come*.

"*Come*, let us talk about these things. Though your sins are like scarlet, they can be as white as snow" (Isaiah 1:18, emphasis added).

"All you who are thirsty, *come* and drink" (Isaiah 55:1, emphasis added).

"*Come* to me all, all of you who are tired and have heavy loads, and I will give you rest" (Matthew 11:28, emphasis added).

God is a God who invites. God is a God who calls.

Your heavenly Father is very fond of you and
only wants to share his love with you.

Jesus said, "Come follow me."

MATTHEW 4:19

The Spirit and the bride say, "Come!" Let
the one who hears this say, "Come!" Let
whoever is thirsty come; whoever wishes
may have the water of life as a free gift.

REVELATION 22:17

"Here I am! I stand at the door and knock. If you
hear my voice and open the door, I will come in
and eat with you, and you will eat with me."

REVELATION 3:20

Sowing Seeds

Want to see a miracle? Plant an act of love heart-deep in a person's life. Nurture it with a smile and a prayer, and watch what happens.

A spouse gets a compliment. A friend receives a bouquet of flowers. A cake is baked and carried next door. A widow is hugged. A child is honored. A preschooler is praised.

Sowing seeds of love and kindness is like sowing beans. You don't know why it works; you just know it does.

Never underestimate the power of a seed.

**Your heart is not large enough to contain
the blessings God wants to give you.**

Plant goodness, harvest the fruit of loyalty,
plow the new ground of knowledge.

HOSEA 10:12

My children, we should love people not only with
words and talk, but by our actions and true caring.

1 JOHN 3:18

The wisdom that comes from God is first
of all pure, then peaceful, gentle, and easy
to please. This wisdom is always ready to
help those who are troubled and to do good
for others. It is always fair and honest.

JAMES 3:17

A Great Big God

*N*ature is God's workshop. The sky is his resume. The universe is his calling card. You want to know who God is? See what he has done. You want to know his power? Take a look at his creation. Curious about his strength? Pay a visit to his home address: 1 Billion Starry Sky Avenue.

He is untainted by the atmosphere of sin, unbridled by the time line of history, unhindered by the weariness of the body.

What controls you doesn't control him. What troubles you doesn't trouble him. What fatigues you doesn't fatigue him. Is an eagle disturbed by traffic? No, he rises above it. Is the whale perturbed by a hurricane? Of course not, he plunges beneath it. Is the lion flustered by the mouse standing directly in his way? No, he steps over it.

How much more is God able to soar above, plunge beneath, and step over the troubles of the earth!

He is a great big God, and he can do all things.

"For God all things are possible."

MATTHEW 19:26

Surely you know. Surely you have heard. The
Lord is the God who lives forever, who created
all the world. He does not become tired or need
to rest. No one can understand how great his
wisdom is. He gives strength to those who are
tired and more power to those who are weak.

ISAIAH 40:28–29

No one is like you, Lord; you are great,
and your name is mighty in power.

JEREMIAH 10:6 NIV

Day 20

You Have Captured God's Heart

*H*ave you ever noticed the way a groom looks at his bride during a wedding? I have. Perhaps it's my vantage point. As the minister of the wedding, I'm positioned next to the groom.

If the light is just so and the angle just right, I can see her reflection in his eyes. And the sight of her reminds him why he is there. His jaw relaxes and his forced smile softens. He forgets he's wearing a tux. When he sees her, any thought of escape becomes a joke. It's written all over his face: "Who could bear to live without this bride?"

And such are precisely the feelings of Jesus. Look long enough into the eyes of our Savior, and there, too, you will see a bride.

And who is this bride for whom Jesus longs? You are. You have captured the heart of God.

God knows your entire story, from first word to final breath, and with clear assessment declares, "You are mine."

As a man rejoices over his new wife,
so your God will rejoice over you.

ISAIAH 62:5

You are altogether beautiful.

SONG OF SONGS 4:7 NIV

God has poured out his love to fill our
hearts. He gave us his love through the
Holy Spirit, whom God has given to us.

ROMANS 5:5

Day 21

What Are Your Strengths?

*T*here are some things we want to do but simply aren't equipped to accomplish. I, for example, have the desire to sing. Singing for others would give me wonderful satisfaction. The problem is, it wouldn't give the same satisfaction to my audience.

Paul gave good advice in Romans 12:3: "Have a sane estimate of your capabilities" (PHILLIPS).

In other words, be aware of your strengths. When you teach, do people listen? When you lead, do people follow? When you administer, do things improve? Where are you most productive? Identify your strengths, and then major in them. Failing to focus on your strengths may prevent you from accomplishing the unique tasks God has called you to do.

Do what you can, and trust God to take care of the rest.

God planned and packed you on purpose for his purpose. You are heaven's custom design.

We all have different gifts, each of which
came because of the grace God gave us.

ROMANS 12:6

She did what she could.

MARK 14:8 NIV

Lord, tell me your ways. Show me how to live.
Guide me in your truth, and teach me, my
God, my Savior. I trust you all day long.

PSALM 25:4–5

When God
made you,
the angels

stood in
awe and
declared,
"We've never
seen one like
that before."
And they never
will again.

Day 22

You're Something Special

We want to know how long God's love will endure. Not just on Sundays when my shoes are shined and my hair is fixed. Not when I'm peppy and positive and ready to tackle world hunger. Not then. I know how he feels about me then. Even I like me then.

I want to know how he feels about me when I snap at anything that moves, when my thoughts are gutter-level, when my tongue is sharp enough to slice a rock. How does he feel about me then?

Can anything separate us from the love Christ has for us?

God answered our question before we asked it. So we'd see his answer, he lit the sky with a star. So we'd hear it, he filled the night with a choir. And so we'd believe it, he did what no man had ever dreamed God would do: he became flesh and dwelt among us.

He placed his hand on the shoulder of humanity and said, "You're something special."

You do not need to win his love. You already have it. And since you can't win it, you can't lose it.

Nothing . . . in the whole world will ever be
able to separate us from the love of God.

ROMANS 8:39

"I give them eternal life, and they shall never perish;
no one will snatch them out of my hand."

JOHN 10:28 NIV

How priceless is your unfailing love, O God!
People take refuge in the shadow of your wings.

PSALM 36:7 NIV

God is God.
He knows what
he is doing. You
can trust his
heart.

My Prayer

Jesus Understands

*J*esus knows how you feel. You're under pressure at work? Jesus knows how you feel. You've got more to do than is humanly possible? So did he. People take more from you than they give? Jesus understands. Your toddlers won't listen? Your teenagers won't try? Jesus knows how you feel.

You are precious to him. So precious that he became like you so that you would come to him.

When you struggle, he listens. When you yearn, he responds. When you question, he hears. He has been there.

He understands, and he is with you.

When you turn to him *for* help, he runs to you *to* help. Why? He knows how you feel. He's been there.

He took our suffering on him
and felt our pain for us.

ISAIAH 53:4

"Don't worry, because I am with you. Don't
be afraid, because I am your God. I will make
you strong and will help you; I will support
you with my right hand that saves you."

ISAIAH 41:10

You have recorded my troubles. You
have kept a list of my tears.

PSALM 56:8

Day 24

You're at Home with God

God wants to be your dwelling place. He has no interest in being a weekend getaway or a Sunday bungalow or a summer cottage. Don't consider using God as a vacation cabin or an eventual retirement home. He wants you under his roof now and always. He wants to be your mailing address, your point of reference; he wants to be your home.

For many, this is a new thought. We think of God as a deity to discuss, not a place to dwell. We think of God as a mysterious miracle worker, not a house to live in. We think of God as a creator to call on, not a home to reside in. But our Father wants to be much more. He wants to be the one in whom "we live and move and have our being" (Acts 17:28 NIV).

As you make a home for those you love, remember your true home—with God—and invite them in.

**If we give gifts to show our love,
how much more would he?**

Jesus answered him, "If anyone loves me,
he will keep my word, and my Father
will love him, and we will come to him
and make our home with him."

JOHN 14:23 ESV

Because of his love, God had already decided to make
us his own children through Jesus Christ. That was
what he wanted and what pleased him, and it brings
praise to God because of his wonderful grace.

EPHESIANS 1:5-6

I ask only one thing from the LORD. This is
what I want: Let me live in the LORD's house
all my life. Let me see the LORD's beauty and
look with my own eyes at his Temple.

PSALM 27:4

Day 25

Ready to Comfort

*M*y child's feelings are hurt. I tell her she's special. My child is injured. I do whatever it takes to make her feel better. My child is afraid. I won't go to sleep until she feels safe.

I'm not a hero. I'm a parent. When a child hurts, parents do what comes naturally. They help.

Why don't I let my Father do for me what I am more than willing to do for my own children?

I'm learning. Being a parent is teaching me that when I am criticized, injured, or afraid, there is One who is ready to comfort me. There is One who will hold me until I'm better, help me until I can live with the hurt, and who won't go to sleep when I'm afraid of waking up and seeing the dark. Ever.

You have a God who hears you, the power of love behind you,
the Holy Spirit within you, and all of heaven ahead of you.

He comforts us every time we have trouble, so
when others have trouble, we can comfort them.

2 CORINTHIANS 1:4

The name of the LORD is a strong fortress;
the godly run to him and are safe.

PROVERBS 18:10 NLT

"I will ask the Father, and He will give you another
Helper, so that He may be with you forever."

JOHN 14:16 NASB

You are who God

says you are . . .

his honored child.

Day 26

True Courage

*T*herefore, there is now no condemnation for those who are in Christ Jesus" (Romans 8:1 NIV). "[God] justifies those who have faith in Jesus" (Romans 3:26 NIV). For those in Christ, these promises are not only a source of joy, they are also the foundations of true courage. (And let's face it: motherhood takes all kinds of courage.) These promises are your guarantee that your mistakes, your missteps, and your sins will be filtered through, hidden in, and screened out by the sacrifice of Jesus. When God looks at you, he doesn't see you; he sees the one who surrounds you. That means that failure is not a concern for you. Your victory is secure. How could you not be courageous? God will not fail you.

He who was perfect gave that perfect record to you, and your imperfect record was given to him.

God's dream is to make you right with him.

So be strong and courageous! Do not be afraid
and do not panic before them. For the LORD
your God will personally go ahead of you.
He will neither fail you nor abandon you.

DEUTERONOMY 31:6 NLT

Christ had no sin, but God made him become sin so
that in Christ we could become right with God.

2 CORINTHIANS 5:21

Therefore he is able to save completely those
who come to God through him, because he
always lives to intercede for them.

HEBREWS 7:25 NIV

You cannot find

a place where

God is not.

My Prayer

_____

_____

_____

_____

_____

_____

_____

_____

_____

Ask Boldly

*J*esus tells us, "Pray then like this: 'Our Father who is in heaven, hallowed be your name. Your kingdom come.'"

When you say, "Your kingdom come," you are inviting the Messiah himself to walk into your world. "Come, my King! Take your throne in our land. Be present in my heart. Be present in my home. Come into my marriage. Be Lord of my family, my fears, and my doubts." This is no feeble request; it's a bold appeal for God to occupy every corner of your life.

And who are you to ask such a thing? Who are you to ask God to take control of your world? You are his child, for heaven's sake! And so you ask boldly.

He lives to hear your heartbeat.
He loves to hear your prayers.

Let us, then, feel very sure that we can come
before God's throne where there is grace.

HEBREWS 4:16

The LORD is close to everyone who prays to
him, to all who truly pray to him.

PSALM 145:18

I call to you, God, and you answer me.

PSALM 17:6

Serving Him

Martha was worried about something good. She was having Jesus over for dinner. She was literally serving God. Her aim was to please Jesus. But she made a common yet dangerous mistake. As she began to work for him, her work became more important than her Lord. What began as a way to serve Jesus, slowly and subtly became a way to serve self. She had forgotten that the meal was to honor Jesus, not Martha.

It's easy to forget who is the servant and who is to be served.

The tasks are so often thankless, and a little praise would go such a long way. But earthly praise quickly fades. Seek his praise—his presence—instead.

God has enough grace to solve every dilemma you face, wipe every tear you cry, and answer every question you ask.

Martha was distracted with much serving. . . . Jesus answered and said to her, "Mary has chosen that good part, which will not be taken away from her."

LUKE 10:40–42 NKJV

Come near to God, and God will come near to you.

JAMES 4:8

Your word is like a lamp for my feet and a light for my path.

PSALM 119:105

Let God have you, and let God love you—and don't be surprised if your heart begins to hear music you've never heard and your feet learn to dance as never before.

Day 29

One Day . . .

*F*or all we don't know about the next life, this much is certain: The day Christ comes will be a day of reward. Those who went unknown on earth will be known in heaven. Those who never heard the cheers of others will hear the cheers of angels. Those who missed the blessing of a father will hear the blessing of their heavenly Father. The small will be great. The forgotten will be remembered. The unnoticed will be crowned, and the faithful will be honored.

The winner's circle isn't reserved for a handful of the elite but for a heaven full of God's children who "will receive the crown of life that the Lord has promised to those who love him" (James 1:12 NIV). The days may seem long. But one day, Mom, you will receive your reward.

God never said the journey would be easy, but he did say that the arrival would be worthwhile.

The Lord will reward each one for whatever
good they do, whether they are slave or free.

EPHESIANS 6:8 NIV

The Spirit himself bears witness with our spirit that we
are children of God, and if children, then heirs—heirs of
God and fellow heirs with Christ, provided we suffer with
him in order that we may also be glorified with him.

ROMANS 8:16–17 ESV

Now, a crown is being held for me—a crown for being right
with God. The Lord, the judge who judges rightly, will give
the crown to me on that day—not only to me but to all
those who have waited with love for him to come again.

2 TIMOTHY 4:8

Day 30

A Burst of Love

ometimes God is so touched by what he sees that he gives us what we need and not simply that for which we ask.

It's a good thing. For who ever would have thought to ask God for what he gives? Which of us would have dared to say: "God, would you please hang yourself on a tool of torture as a substitution for every mistake I have ever committed?" And then have the audacity to add: "And after you forgive me, could you prepare me a place in your house to live forever?"

If that wasn't enough: "And would you please live within me and protect me and guide me and bless me with more than I could ever deserve?"

Honestly, would we have the chutzpah to ask for that?

Jesus already knows the cost of grace. He already knows the price of forgiveness. But he offers it anyway. Love bursts his heart.

"Seek God's kingdom, and all your
other needs will be met as well."

LUKE 12:31

"Greater love has no one than this: to lay
down one's life for one's friends."

JOHN 15:13 NIV

This is how God showed his love to us: He sent his
one and only Son into the world so that we could
have life through him. This is what real love is: It is
not our love for God; it is God's love for us. He sent
his Son to die in our place to take away our sins.

1 JOHN 4:9–10

You are valuable
to him . . . not
because of what
you do but
simply because
you are.

My Prayer

Day 31

God Is for You

*G*od is *for* you. Turn to the sidelines; that's God cheering your run. Look past the finish line; that's God applauding your steps. Listen for him in the bleachers shouting your name. Too tired to continue? He'll carry you. Too discouraged to fight? He's picking you up. God is for you.

God is for *you*. Had he a calendar, your birthday would be circled. If he drove a car, your name would be on his bumper. If there's a tree in heaven, he's carved your name in the bark.

"Can a mother forget the baby at her breast and have no compassion on the child she has borne?" God asks in Isaiah 49:15 (NIV). What a bizarre question. Can you imagine feeding your infant and then later asking, "What was that baby's name?" No. I've seen you care for your young. You stroke the hair, you touch the face, you sing the name over and over. Can a mother forget? No way. But "even if she could forget, . . . I will not forget you," God pledges (Isaiah 49:15 NCV).

You will rest in his love; he will sing
and be joyful about you.

ZEPHANIAH 3:17

God is the one who saves me; I will trust him
and not be afraid. The LORD, the LORD gives me
strength and makes me sing. He has saved me.

ISAIAH 12:2

"I, the LORD, made you, and I will not forget you."

ISAIAH 44:21 NLT

The maker of the stars would rather die for you than live without you.

Day 32

What's Right

*Y*ou get impatient with your own life, trying to master a habit or control a sin—and in your frustration, you begin to wonder where the power of God is. Be patient. God is using today's difficulties to strengthen you for tomorrow. He is *equipping* you. The God who makes things grow will help you bear fruit.

Dwell on the fact that God lives within you. Think about the power that gives you life. The realization that God is dwelling within you may change the things you want to do today.

Do what is right today, whatever it is. Maybe no one else is doing what's right, but you do what's right. You be kind. You take a stand. You be true. After all, regardless of what you do, God does what is right: he saves you with his grace.

God has not only read your story, he wrote
it. His perspective is different, and his
purpose is clear: to rescue you.

God has chosen you and made you his holy
people. He loves you. So you should always
clothe yourselves with mercy, kindness,
humility, gentleness, and patience.

COLOSSIANS 3:12

Think about the things that are good and worthy of
praise. Think about the things that are true and honorable
and right and pure and beautiful and respected.

PHILIPPIANS 4:8

We must not become tired of doing good. We will receive our
harvest of eternal life at the right time if we do not give up.

GALATIANS 6:9

A Mother's Prayers

*N*ever underestimate the ponderings of a Christian mom. Never underestimate the power that comes when a mother pleads with God on behalf of a child. Who knows how many prayers are being answered right now because of the faithful ponderings of a mom ten or twenty years ago? God listens to thoughtful mothers.

Praying for our children is a noble task. If what we are doing, in this fast-paced society, is taking us away from prayer time for our children, we're doing too much. There is nothing more special, more precious, than the time a mom spends struggling and pondering with God on behalf of a child.

A mother will go to any length to find
her own child. So will God.

All your children will be taught by the
LORD, and they will have much peace.

ISAIAH 54:13

Do not worry about anything, but pray and ask God
for everything you need, always giving thanks.

PHILIPPIANS 4:6

And this is the boldness we have in God's presence: that
if we ask God for anything that agrees with what he
wants, he hears us. If we know he hears us every time
we ask him, we know we have what we ask from him.

1 JOHN 5:14–15

He Knows Your Name

*T*he Shepherd knows his sheep. He calls them by name.

When we see a crowd, we see exactly that—a crowd. We see people—not persons, but people. A herd of humans. A flock of faces. That's what we see.

But not so with the Shepherd. To him every face is different. Every face is a story. Every face is a child. Every child has a name.

The Shepherd knows his sheep. He knows each one by name. The Shepherd knows you. He knows your name. And he will never forget it.

God's love for you is not dependent on how you look, how you think, how you act, or how perfect you are. His love is absolutely nonnegotiable and nonreturnable.

"I am the good shepherd. I know my
sheep, and my sheep know me."

JOHN 10:14

LORD, you have examined me and know all about
me. You know when I sit down and when I get up.
You know my thoughts before I think them.

PSALM 139:1 2

The LORD is good, a stronghold in the day of
trouble; he knows those who take refuge in him.

NAHUM 1:7 ESV

God's Spirit whispers,
"You are mine, and
no one can take you."

Day 35

God's Great Gifts

*W*hy did he do it? A shack would have sufficed, but he gave us a mansion. Did he have to give the birds a song and the mountains a peak? Was he required to put stripes on the zebra and the hump on the camel? Why wrap creation in such splendor? Why go to such trouble to give such gifts?

Why do you? I've seen you searching for a gift. I've seen you stalking the malls and walking the aisles. I'm not talking about the obligatory gifts. I'm talking about that extra-special gift. You do it to hear those words of disbelief, "You did this for *me*?"

That's why you do it. And that is why God did it. For you.

God could have left the world flat and gray, but he didn't.
He splashed orange in the sunrise and cast the sky in blue.
Why give a flower fragrance? Why give food its taste?
Could it be that he loves to see that look upon your face?

Thanks be to God for his gift that
is too wonderful for words.

2 CORINTHIANS 9:15

When I consider your heavens, the work of your
fingers, the moon and the stars, which you have set
in place, what is mankind that you are mindful of
them, human beings that you care for them?

PSALM 8:3-4 NIV

He has made everything beautiful in its time. He has
also set eternity in the human heart; yet no one can
fathom what God has done from beginning to end.

ECCLESIASTES 3:11 NIV

We forget how significant one touch can be . . . but aren't we glad Jesus doesn't?

My Prayer

Your Defender

*H*ere is a big question. What is God doing when we are in a bind? When the lifeboat springs a leak? When the rip cord snaps? When the last penny is gone before the last bill is paid?

I know what we are doing. Nibbling on our fingernails like corn on the cob. Pacing floors. Pulling our hair.

But what does God do?

He fights for us. He steps into the ring and points us to our corner and takes over. "Remain calm; the LORD will fight for you" (Exodus 14:14).

His job is to fight. Our job is to trust.

Just trust. Not direct. Or question. Our job is to pray and wait. He will take care of the rest.

The Christ of the galaxies is the Christ of your days. The Starmaker manages your schedule. Relax. You have a friend in high places.

He is my defender; I will not be defeated.

PSALM 62:6

You only need to remain calm; the
LORD will fight for you.

EXODUS 14:14

Stop striving and know that I am God.

PSALM 46:10 NASB

One of a Kind

*I*n my closet hangs a sweater that I seldom wear. It is too small. I should throw that sweater away. But *love* won't let me.

It's the creation of a devoted mother expressing her love. Each strand was chosen with care. It is valuable not because of its function but because of its maker.

That must have been what the psalmist had in mind when he wrote, "You knit me together in my mother's womb" (Psalm 139:13 NIV).

Think on those words. You were knitted together. You aren't an accident. You weren't mass-produced. You aren't an assembly-line product.

You were deliberately planned, specifically gifted, and lovingly positioned on this earth by the Master Craftsman. In a system that ranks the value of a human by the figures in her salary or the shape of her legs, let me tell you something: Jesus' plan is a reason for joy!

You made my whole being; you formed
me in my mother's body.

PSALM 139:13

You made me and formed me with your hands. Give
me understanding so I can learn your commands.

PSALM 119:73

And who knows whether you have not come
to the kingdom for such a time as this?

ESTHER 4:14 ESV

Gifts of Love

*E*ver feel like you have nothing? Just look at the gifts God has given you:

He has sent his angels to care for you, his Holy Spirit to dwell in you, his church to encourage you, and his Word to guide you.

Anytime you speak, he listens; make a request and he responds.

He will never let you be tempted too much or stumble too far.

Let a tear appear on your cheek, and he is there to wipe it.

Let a love sonnet appear on your lips, and he is there to hear it.

As much as you want to see him, he wants to see you more.

You have been chosen by Christ. He has claimed you as his beloved.

Flooded by emotion, overcome by pride, the Lord
of all creation turns to us, one by one, and
says, "You are my child. I love you dearly."

Every good action and every
perfect gift is from God.

JAMES 1:17

Trust in the LORD with all your heart; do not depend
on your own understanding. Seek his will in all
you do, and he will show you which path to take.

PROVERBS 3:5–6 NLT

My God will supply every need of yours
according to his riches in glory in Christ Jesus.

PHILIPPIANS 4:19 ESV

Be kind to yourself.
After all, God thinks
you're worth
his kindness.

Day 39

God's Name in Your Heart

*W*hen you are confused about the future, go to your *Jehovah-raah,* your caring shepherd. When you are anxious about provision, talk to *Jehovah-jireh,* the Lord who provides. Are your challenges too great? Seek the help of *Jehovah-shalom,* the Lord is peace. Is your body sick? Are your emotions weak? *Jehovah-rophe,* the Lord who heals you, will see you now. Do you feel like a soldier stranded behind enemy lines? Take refuge in *Jehovah-nissi,* the Lord my banner.

Meditating on the names of God reminds you of the character of God. Take these names and bury them in your heart.

God is the shepherd who guides, the Lord who provides, the voice who brings peace in the storm, the physician who heals the sick, and the banner that guides the soldier.

God is *in* you. . . . He will do what you cannot.

118

The name of the LORD is a strong tower;
the righteous run to it and are safe.

PROVERBS 18:10 NKJV

For to us a child is born, to us a son is given, and
the government will be on his shoulders. And
he will be called Wonderful Counselor, Mighty
God, Everlasting Father, Prince of Peace.

ISAIAH 9:6 NIV

The LORD is my shepherd, I lack nothing.

PSALM 23:1 NIV

God calls you to himself and invites you to take a permanent place at his table.

My Prayer

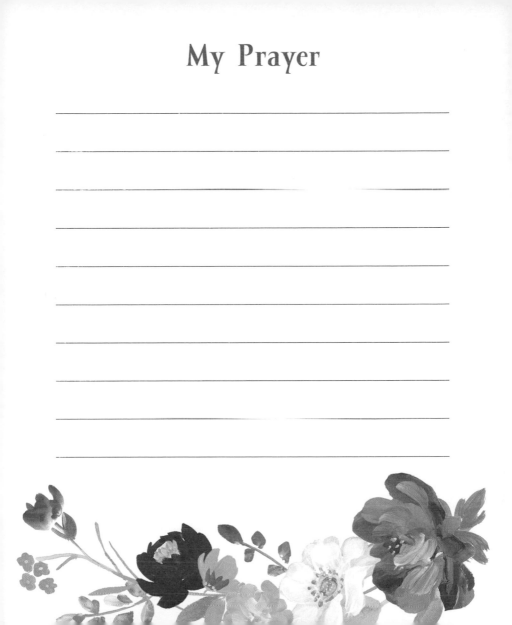

Day 40

Your Whispering Thoughts

*I*magine considering every moment as a potential time of communion with God. By the time your life is over, you will have spent six months at stoplights, eight months opening junk mail, a year and a half looking for lost stuff (double that number in my case), and a whopping five years standing in various lines.

Why don't you give these moments to God? Simple phrases such as "Thank you, Father" and "You are my resting place, Jesus" can turn a commute into a pilgrimage. You needn't leave your office or kneel in your kitchen. Just pray where you are. Let the kitchen become a cathedral or the car a chapel. Give God your whispering thoughts.

Some things only a mom can know. How many days are left in the semester? The time it takes to drive from piano lesson to Little League practice? She knows. And she knows she can give all those moments to God.

God, examine me and know my heart; test
me and know my anxious thoughts.

PSALM 139:23

Morning by morning he wakens me and opens
my understanding to his will. The Sovereign
LORD has spoken to me, and I have listened.

ISAIAH 50:4–5 NLT

Truly my soul finds rest in God; my salvation comes
from him. Truly he is my rock and my salvation;
he is my fortress, I will never be shaken.

PSALM 62:1–2 NIV

Day 41

The God Who Follows

O ur God is the God who follows. Have you sensed him following you? He is the one who came to seek and save the lost. Have you sensed him seeking you?

Have you felt his presence through the kindness of a stranger? Through the majesty of a sunset or the mystery of romance? Through the question of a child or the commitment of a spouse? Through a word well spoken or a touch well timed, have you sensed him?

God gives us himself. Even when we choose our hovel over his house and our trash over his grace, still he follows. Never forcing us. Never leaving us. Patiently persistent. Faithfully present. He uses all his power to convince us that he can be trusted to lead us home.

God wants you to know he is in the midst of your world.
Wherever you are as you read these words, he is present.
He is as near to you on Monday as he is on Sunday.

"The Son of Man came to find
lost people and save them."

LUKE 19:10

You will teach me how to live a holy life.
Being with you will fill me with joy; at your
right hand I will find pleasure forever.

PSALM 16:11

"I will be with you always, even
until the end of this age."

MATTHEW 28:20

A Mother's Hands

*W*hat if someone were to film a documentary about your hands? What would we see? As with all of us, the film would begin with an infant's fist, then a close-up of a tiny hand wrapped around Mommy's finger. Then what? Holding on to a chair as you learned to walk?

Were you to show the documentary to your friends, you'd be proud of certain moments: your hands extending with a gift, placing a ring on another's finger, doctoring a wound, preparing a meal. And then there would be other scenes. Hands taking more often than giving, demanding instead of offering.

Oh, the power of our hands. Leave them unmanaged, and they become weapons. But manage them, and our hands become instruments of grace—not just tools in the hands of God, but God's very hands.

Let your gentleness be evident to all.

PHILIPPIANS 4:5 NIV

Whatever you do, work at it with all your
heart, as working for the Lord.

COLOSSIANS 3:23 NIV

"When you give to someone in need, don't let
your left hand know what your right hand is
doing. Give your gifts in private, and your Father,
who sees everything, will reward you."

MATTHEW 6:3-4 NLT

A little rain can straighter a flower stem. A little love can change a life.

Adventure Is Calling

*J*esus says the options are clear. On one side is the voice of safety. You can build a fire in the hearth, stay inside, and stay warm and dry, right? You can't fall if you don't take a stand, right? You can't lose your balance if you never climb, right? So don't try it. Take the safe route.

Or you can hear the voice of adventure—God's adventure. Instead of building a fire in your hearth, build a fire in your heart. Follow God's impulses. Adopt the child. Move overseas. Teach the class. Run for office. Make a difference. After all, God made you a mom. And that's what moms do.

God has a great race for you to run. Under
his care you will go where you've never been
and serve in ways you've never dreamed.

The Lord is my light and my
salvation—whom shall I fear?

PSALM 27:1 NIV

"Call to me and I will answer you and tell you great
and unsearchable things you do not know."

JEREMIAH 33:3 NIV

Jesus called out to them, "Come, follow me, and
I will show you how to fish for people!"

MATTHEW 4:19 NLT

Sweeter After a Rest

When I was ten years old, my mother enrolled me in piano lessons. Spending thirty minutes every afternoon tethered to a piano bench was torture.

Some of the music, though, I learned to enjoy. I hammered the staccatos. I belabored the crescendos. But there was one instruction in the music I could never obey to my teacher's satisfaction. The *rest*. The zigzagged command to do nothing. What sense does that make? Why sit at the piano and pause when you can pound?

"Because," my teacher patiently explained, "music is always sweeter after a rest."

It didn't make sense to me then, but now the words ring with divine wisdom. Life is sweeter after a rest.

Slow down, and God will bring rest to your mind,
to your body, and most of all to your soul.

In six days the LORD made everything. . . .
On the seventh day he rested.

EXODUS 20:11

He lets me rest in green pastures.
He leads me to calm water.

PSALM 23:2

Let all that I am wait quietly before
God, for my hope is in him.

PSALM 62:5 NLT

God knows you better
than you know you and
has reached his verdict:
he loves you still.

My Prayer

Day 45

Your Own Personal Blessing

God will praise each one of them. What an incredible sentence. Not "the best of them" nor "a few of them" nor "the achievers among them," but "God will praise each one of them" (1 Corinthians 4:5).

You won't be left out. God will see to that. In fact, God himself will give the praise. When it comes to giving recognition, God does not delegate the job. Michael doesn't hand out the crowns. Gabriel doesn't speak on behalf of the throne. God himself does the honors. You might feel unnoticed here, but God himself will praise you as his child.

And what's more, the praise is personal! Awards aren't given a nation at a time, a church at a time, or a generation at a time. The crowns are given one at a time. God himself will look you in the eye and bless you with the words, "Well done, good and faithful servant!" (Matthew 25:23 NIV).

As boldly as the center beam of the cross
proclaims God's holiness, the crossbeam declares
his love. And, oh, how wide his love reaches!

136

God will praise each one of them.

1 CORINTHIANS 4:5

God's eye is on those who respect him,
the ones who are looking for his love.
He's ready to come to their rescue.

PSALM 33:18–19 THE MESSAGE

The Lord searches all the earth for people who
have given themselves completely to him.

2 CHRONICLES 16:9

When you do the

most what you do

the best, you put

a smile on

God's face.

Love Lasts

*C*an anything make me stop loving you?" God asks. "Watch me speak your language, sleep on your earth, and feel your hurts. Behold the maker of sight and sound as he sneezes, coughs, and blows his nose. You wonder if I understand how you feel? Look into the dancing eyes of the kid in Nazareth; that's God walking to school. Ponder the toddler at Mary's table; that's God spilling his milk.

"You wonder how long my love will last? Find your answer on a splintered cross, on a craggy hill. That's me you see up there, your Maker, your God, nail-stabbed and bleeding. Covered in spit and sin-soaked.

"That's your sin I'm feeling. That's your death I'm dying. That's your resurrection I'm living. That's how much I love you."

Your place in heaven was more important to Christ than his place in heaven, so he gave up his so you could have yours.

God shows his great love for us in this way:
Christ died for us while we were still sinners.

ROMANS 5:8

God is love.

1 JOHN 4:8

Thank the LORD because he is good.
His love continues forever.

1 CHRONICLES 16:34

Just Pray

D o you want to know how to deepen your prayer life? Pray. Don't prepare to pray. Just pray. Don't read about prayer. Just pray. Don't attend a lecture on prayer or engage in discussion about prayer. Just pray.

Posture, tone, and place are personal matters. Select the form that works for you. But don't think about it too much. Don't be so concerned about wrapping the gift that you never give it. Better to pray awkwardly than not at all.

And if you feel you should only pray when inspired, that's okay. Just see to it that you are inspired every day.

If you want to touch God's heart, use the
name he loves to hear. Call him "Abba."

Anyone who is having troubles should pray.
Anyone who is happy should sing praises.

JAMES 5:13

Look to the LORD and his strength;
seek his face always.

1 CHRONICLES 16:11 NIV

Pray in the Spirit at all times with all kinds of
prayers, asking for everything you need.

EPHESIANS 6:18

His Joy

God sees you with the eyes of a Father. He sees your defects, errors, and blemishes. But he also sees your value.

What did Jesus know that enabled him to do what he did?

Here's part of the answer: He knew the value of people. He knew that each human being is a treasure. And because he did, people were not a source of stress but a source of joy.

You matter to the Savior. You are his joy.

God loves to be with the people he loves.

"God does not see the same way people
see. People look at the outside of a person,
but the LORD looks at the heart."

1 SAMUEL 16:7

The LORD loves you.

DEUTERONOMY 7:8 NLT

He led me to a place of safety; he rescued
me because he delights in me.

PSALM 18:19 NLT

Day 49

Just the Way You Are

*I*f a sentence or two could capture God's desire for each of us, it might read like this:

God loves you just the way you are, but he refuses to leave you that way. He wants you to be just like Jesus.

God loves you just the way you are. If you think his love for you would be stronger if your faith were stronger, you are wrong. If you think his love would be deeper if your thoughts were deeper, wrong again. Don't confuse God's love with others' love. The love of people often increases with performance and decreases with mistakes. Not so with God's love. He loves you right where you are. Just as you are.

God began doing a good work in you,
and I am sure he will continue it until it is
finished when Jesus Christ comes again.

PHILIPPIANS 1:6

Great is the LORD, who delights in
blessing his servant with peace!

PSALM 35:27 NLT

Love is patient and kind. Love is not jealous, it does
not brag, and it is not proud. Love is not rude, is not
selfish, and does not get upset with others. Love does
not count up wrongs that have been done. Love takes
no pleasure in evil but rejoices over the truth. Love
patiently accepts all things. It always trusts, always
hopes, and always endures. Love never ends.

1 CORINTHIANS 13:4-8

God has a relentless, undying, unfathomable, unquenchable love for you from which you cannot be separated. Ever! No matter what!

The Best Is Yet to Be

*P*arents are fond of giving their children special names. Princess. Tiger. Sweetheart. Bubba. Angel.

Isn't it incredible to think that God has saved a name just for you? One you don't even know? We've always assumed that the name we got is the name we will keep. Not so. The road ahead is so bright that a fresh name is needed. Your eternity is so special that no common name will do.

So God has one reserved just for you. There is more to your life than you ever thought. There is more to your story than what you have read.

And so I plead: be there when God whispers your name.

**God already knows you! He tattooed your name
on the palm of his hand (Isaiah 49:16).**

"I will also give to each one who wins the victory
a white stone with a new name written on it."

REVELATION 2:17

Now this is what the LORD says. . . . "Don't
be afraid, because I have saved you. I have
called you by name, and you are mine."

ISAIAH 43:1

"Here I am!"

ISAIAH 6:8 ESV

With perfect knowledge

of your imperfect life,

God signed on.

My Prayer

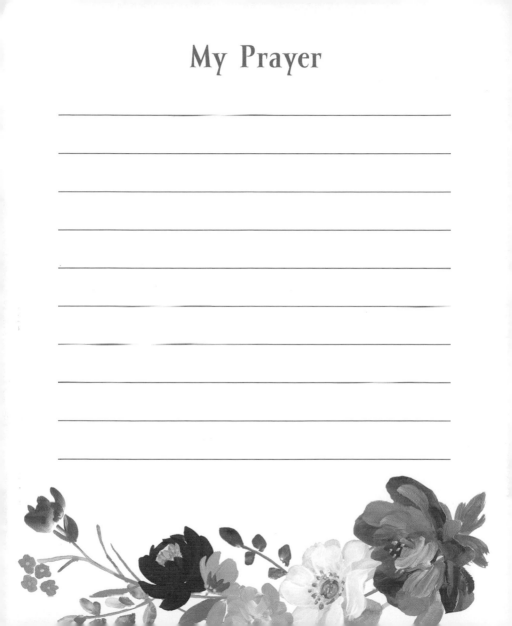

About the Author

*S*ince entering the ministry in 1978, Max Lucado has served churches in Miami, Florida; Rio de Janeiro, Brazil; and San Antonio, Texas. He currently serves as Teaching Minister of Oak Hills Church in San Antonio. He is the recipient of the 2021 ECPA Pinnacle Award for his outstanding contribution to the publishing industry and society at large. He is America's bestselling inspirational author with more than 145 million products in print.

Visit his website at MaxLucado.com

Facebook.com/MaxLucado

Instagram.com/MaxLucado

Twitter.com/MaxLucado

Youtube.com/MaxLucadoOfficial

The Max Lucado Encouraging Word Podcast